CONTENTS

HARK THE GLAD SOUND!
THE SAVIOUR COMES

After the birth of Jesus, the world was never the same again. But every generation must discover the good news for itself.

The last of his parents' twenty children, Philip Doddridge grew up in a house in the narrow streets of old London. He learned the Bible at his mother's knee, helped by the pictures on the Dutch tiles around their big fireplace.

At that time only members of the Church of England could study at Oxford or Cambridge Universities, and after becoming a Congregational pastor himself, Dr Doddridge set up a 'Dissenting Academy' in Northampton and trained over 200 students, most as preachers. He believed in changing an unjust society — but that only changed people could do the job.

He wrote *The Rise and Progress of Religion in the Soul*, and one whose life was changed by reading it was young William Wilberforce. His scoffing at the 'Methodists' turned to admiration, firm Christian commitment, and political reform including his anti-slavery campaigns.

This hymn, called 'Christ's message', is based on a startling sermon in Luke chapter 4, which Jesus preached at Nazareth, and accompanied one of Doddridge's own sermons at Northampton. It is not only for the Advent season, but its ringing challenge prepares us for the festival where freedom is announced — from chains both seen and unseen.

1

Hark the glad sound! the Saviour comes,
The Saviour promised long;
Let every heart prepare a throne
And every voice a song.

CHRISTMAS CAROLS

AND THEIR STORIES

compiled by Christopher Idle

SANDY
LANE
BOOKS

Text copyright © 1988 Christopher Idle
This edition copyright © 1988 Lion Publishing

Published by
Sandy Lane Books
Sandy Lane West, Oxford, England
ISBN 0 7459 4002 1
Albatross Books Pty Ltd
PO Box 320, Sutherland, NSW 2232, Australia
ISBN 0 7324 1340 0

First edition 1988
This edition 1995
10 9 8 7 6 5 4 3 2 1 0

In this collection, the word 'carol' is used in its widest
sense to include many kinds of seasonal songs and hymns.
Other Christmas items may be found in the companion
book, F*amous Hymns and their Stories*.

Acknowledgments
All copyright hymns are reproduced by kind permission of the authors

The photograph of a stained glass window on
page 51 is reproduced by kind permission of
the vicar of Winchelsea Parish Church, Sussex.

Photographs by Susan Griggs Agency, pages 41, 71;
Alistair Duncan, page 37; Sonia Halliday Photographs:
Sonia Halliday, pages 11, 19, 25, 35, 45, 49, 51, 53,
57, 60, 63, 65, 92; David Townsend, pages 9, 55, 87;
ZEFA (UK) Ltd, pages 17, 27, 32, 47, 72, 77, 79, 81,
91 and cover.

A catalogue record for this title is available
from the British Library

Printed and bound in Singapore

2

He comes the prisoners to release
    In Satan's bondage held;
The gates of brass before him burst,
    The iron fetters yield.

3

He comes the broken heart to bind,
    The bleeding soul to cure,
And with the treasures of his grace
    To enrich the humble poor.

4

Our glad hosannas, Prince of peace,
    Thy welcome shall proclaim.
And heaven's eternal arches ring
    With thy beloved name.

PHILIP DODDRIDGE (1702–51)

LITTLE DONKEY

In the story of Jesus as told in the Gospels, the donkey does not come on stage until Palm Sunday, the lead up to Easter. But popular tradition has given him a role in the Christmas story too.

A young schoolteacher from Sunderland submitted this song to a publisher in 1959. Unlike some unsolicited gifts it was instantly appreciated and became a big success, proving popular among all age groups. Many leading pop ballad singers of the 1960s recorded it; junior schools still love it, so the little donkey takes another bow every year.

1

Little donkey, little donkey,
On the dusty road,
Got to keep on plodding onwards
With your precious load.

2

Been a long time, little donkey,
Through the winter's night;
Don't give up now, little donkey,
Bethlehem's in sight.

Ring out those bells tonight,
Bethlehem, Bethlehem!
Follow that star tonight!
Bethlehem, Bethlehem!

3

Little donkey, little donkey,
Had a heavy day;
Little donkey, carry Mary
Safely on her way.
Little donkey, carry Mary
Safely on her way.

ERIC BOSWELL (born 1927)

BEFORE THE MARVEL
OF THIS NIGHT

'What can I say about the Christmas angels that has not been said already?' Former Lutheran pastor Jaroslav Vajda asked himself this question in 1981 when he was invited to contribute something on that theme to an American anthology of art and literature published each year in Minneapolis.

He had often worked with composer Carl Schalk; they knew that choir rehearsals could be both tough and enjoyable. Did the angels, he wondered, do a little preliminary practising for Bethlehem?

That thought prompted these words; the shepherds were treated to the first sample of the celestial song. Professor Schalk came up with the music and the carol was published that year.

Both sets of Jaroslav's grandparents emigrated in the 1880s to America from Slovakia — the eastern part of modern Czechoslovakia. He was born in Ohio but soon learned to love his native heritage, becoming a translator and interpreter of many Slovak hymns and poems. After eighteen years in parish ministry he spent a further twenty-four as a magazine and book editor; he retired to St Louis but is busy writing and helping others to write.

Hymns, he believes, must speak our awareness of a world and a church very different from those of the past. He admits to 'a lifelong struggle with worship', but when reading his own texts finds it difficult to believe that he wrote them! 'That they exist at all is testimony to the grace and leading of God, the giver and blesser of every gift.'

Before the marvel of this night
Adoring, fold your wings and bow;
Then tear the sky apart with light
And with your news the world endow.
  Proclaim the birth of Christ and peace
  That fear and death and sorrow cease:
  Sing peace, sing peace, sing gift of peace,
  Sing peace, sing gift of peace!

2

Awake the sleeping world with song,
This is the day the Lord has made;
Assemble here, celestial throng,
In royal splendour come arrayed.
  Give earth a glimpse of heavenly bliss,
  A teasing taste of what they miss:
  Sing bliss, sing bliss, sing endless bliss,
  Sing bliss, sing endless bliss!

3

The love that we have always known,
Our constant joy and endless light,
Now to the loveless world be shown,
Now break upon its deathly night.
  Into one song compress the love
  That rules our universe above:
  Sing love, sing love, sing God is love,
  Sing love, sing God is love.

JAROSLAV J. VAJDA (born 1919)

IT CAME UPON
THE MIDNIGHT CLEAR

Soon after Charles Dickens published *A Christmas Carol* in England, these verses first saw the light in Massachusetts. They became one of the first American carol-hymns to spread a Christmas message around the world.

Dr Sears was a farmer's son and a descendant of one of the original Pilgrim Fathers. He was writing poems from the age of ten, and loved to recite and even preach in solitude to what he called 'my assembly of elder bushes'.

He scraped together his college fees for studying law and then theology. He belonged to the Unitarians but perhaps was not a very exact one himself, staunchly maintaining 'I believe and preach the divinity of Christ!'

Not many carols of those days were much concerned with peace among people and nations, as this one is. The magazine editor who published it said 'I was very much delighted with it. I always felt that however poor my Christmas sermon may be, the reading and singing of this hymn are enough to make up for all deficiencies.'

Even as he wrote, the author was aware of wars and revolutions in Europe, India and elsewhere. By a sad irony, within ten years the American Civil War had broken out.

1

It came upon the midnight clear
    That glorious song of old,
From angels bending near the earth
    To touch their harps of gold:
'Peace on the earth, goodwill and grace
    From heaven's all-gracious King!'
The world in solemn stillness lay
    To hear the angels sing.

2

Still through the cloven skies they come
    With peaceful wings unfurled,
And still their heavenly music floats
    O'er all the weary world:
Above its sad and lowly plains
    They bend on hovering wing,
And ever o'er its babel sounds
    The blessed angels sing.

3

Yet with the woes of sin and strife
    The world has suffered long;
Beneath the angel-strain have rolled
    Two thousand years of wrong:
And man, at war with man, hears not
    The love-song which they bring;
O hush the noise, ye men of strife,
    And hear the angels sing!

4

For lo! the days are hastening on
    By prophets seen of old,
When with the ever-circling years
    Shall come the time foretold
When peace shall over all the earth
    Its ancient splendours fling,
And the whole world give back the song
    Which now the angels sing.

EDMUND HAMILTON SEARS (1810–76)

SILENT NIGHT

One small boy, on his way to school in wartime Britain, remembers passing German prisoners of war laying cables in the road. They wound them off huge wooden drums; each of their jackets boldly stamped 'P.O.W'.

At Christmas, his parents took the opportunity to invite some of the prisoners to their home. The family was sternly warned not to talk about the war. After Christmas dinner and the exchange of presents they sang carols round the piano. And that is how the compiler of this book remembers two German friends singing in their own language, 'Stille Nacht, Heilige Nacht', while we joined them in our version, singing together words that make for peace.

Text and tune were written for each other in an Alpine village in the Austrian Tyrol; this translation comes mainly from Bishop Young of Florida. Christ the Saviour is needed equally among the mountain snows, the sandy beaches or the city streets.

1

Silent night! Holy night!
All is calm, all is bright,
Round yon virgin mother and child;
Holy infant, so tender and mild,
  Sleep in heavenly peace,
  Sleep in heavenly peace.

2

Silent night! Holy night!
Shepherds quail at the sight;
Glories stream from heaven afar,
Heavenly hosts sing Alleluia!
  Christ the Saviour is born.
  Christ the Saviour is born.

3

Silent night! Holy night!
Son of God, love's pure light
Radiant beams from thy holy face,
With the dawn of redeeming grace,
  Jesus, Lord, at thy birth,
  Jesus, Lord, at thy birth.

JOSEPH MOHR (1792–1848)
translated by JOHN FREEMAN YOUNG (1820–85)

CHILD IN THE MANGER

We owe this hymn to four very different Scots. In the best folk tradition, Alexander Fraser noted down the tune from the singing of a wandering highlander. He named it *Bunessan* after the birthplace of Mary MacDonald, whose Gaelic poems included one about the 'Child of Agh' — meaning power, wonder and joy. And the music perfectly matched this translation made by the editor of the Fifeshire Advertiser, Lachlan Macbean.

Like the American tune for 'Amazing grace' it was sung as a hymn long before the pop music world discovered it and launched it to the top twenty with the words 'Morning has broken'. But these words have belonged to the tune for a hundred years, ever since Macbean's *Songs and Hymns of the Gael* in 1888.

Mary came from a poetic family. She sang while she span, and with a twinkle in her eyes she also composed some satirical verses about tobacco. Her crofter husband, she reckoned, smoked too much. No doubt the other Mary sang as well, of the unique destiny prophesied for her child.

1	*2*	*3*
Child in the manger,	Once the most holy	Prophets foretold him,
Infant of Mary,	Child of salvation	Infant of wonder,
Outcast and stranger,	Gentle and lowly	Angels behold him
Lord of all!	Lived below;	On his throne:
Child who inherits	Now as our glorious	Worthy our Saviour
All our transgressions,	Mighty Redeemer,	Of all our praises;
All our demerits	See him victorious	Happy for ever
On him fall.	O'er each foe.	Are his own.

MARY MACDONALD (1789–1872)

translated by LACHLAN MACBEAN (1853–1931)

THOU WHO WAST RICH

What Frank Houghton lacked in physical fitness he made up for in high spirits and love of adventure.

When he was seventeen, he and his brother Alfred nearly drowned when they were trapped by the incoming tide at Boscombe. Their sister Eileen knew that neither of them could swim; she rushed fully-clothed into the sea to help, rapidly chased by a man who thought she was trying to commit suicide! He dragged an unconscious Alfred out by his hair, and after some delay two more men rescued Frank, who was by then under water.

Some desperate artificial respiration followed, and both boys recovered. Lying exhausted in bed that night, they read from Psalm 40 in *Daily Light*: 'He brought me up out of a horrible pit, and set my feet upon a rock . . . He hath put a new song in my mouth.'

Frank's life was to be full of 'new songs'. He was thrilled to read the life story of Hudson Taylor, founder of the China Inland Mission, though mildly relieved when doctors declared him unfit for travel abroad. But God's call persisted and in 1920 he himself sailed for China.

These were violent and dangerous times. He continued his boyhood habit of putting his thoughts into verse, and wrote this Christmas hymn based on 2 Corinthians, chapter 8, verse 9, while travelling along the mountain tracks of Szechwan in West China with the good news of Christ.

He became a bishop, and led the Mission as General Secretary through some of its toughest years. Later, back in England, he was still writing and singing of Christ until his last illness at Pembury in Kent.

1

Thou who wast rich beyond all splendour,
All for love's sake becamest poor;
Thrones for a manger didst surrender,
Sapphire-paved courts for stable floor:
    Thou who wast rich beyond all splendour,
    All for love's sake becamest poor.

2

Thou who art God beyond all praising,
All for love's sake becamest man;
Stooping so low, but sinners raising
Heavenward by thine eternal plan:
    Thou who art God beyond all praising,
    All for love's sake becamest man.

3

Thou who art love beyond all telling,
Saviour and King, we worship thee;
Emmanuel, within us dwelling,
Make us what thou wouldst have us be:
    Thou who art love beyond all telling,
    Saviour and King, we worship thee.

FRANK HOUGHTON (1894–1972)

A CHILD
THIS DAY IS BORN

The west country of England can claim credit for this traditional carol; beyond that, and its first known printing in 1822, it is one of many Christmas songs going back centuries, whose authors' names are lost to us for ever.

The tune *Sandys* has been used to accompany many other words in our hymn books, but it made its first recorded appearance with the original twenty-one verses of this text. It provides a distinctively majestic and stately music for the royal flavour of the theme.

William Sandys, who discovered it, was a London solicitor with a talent for mental arithmetic and playing the cello. He studied the old Cornish language and wrote, among other topics, on the history of the violin and of Christmas itself.

But his enduring work was the rescuing of old carols from oblivion. Carol-singing has had its ups and downs; Sandys considered that it survived in the northern counties of England and some of the Midlands, but that it seemed 'to get more neglected every year'.

If that was true, this antiquary and collector did much to reverse the trend. These words do more than revive a tradition; they celebrate an imperishable kingdom.

A child this day is born,
A child of high renown;
Most worthy of a sceptre,
A sceptre and a crown.
Glad tidings sing to all,
Glad tidings sing we may;
Because the King of all kings
Was born on Christmas Day.

2

These tidings shepherds heard
While watching o'er their fold
'Twas by an angel unto them
That night revealed and told.

3

They praised the Lord our God
And our celestial King;
All glory be in Paradise,
This heavenly host do sing.

4

All glory be to God
Who sitteth yet on high,
With praises and with triumph great
And joyful melody.

TRADITIONAL ENGLISH

ANGELS FROM
THE REALMS OF GLORY

James Montgomery was just the man to see
Christmas as a good news story. He was a Scottish journalist
who edited the *Sheffield Iris* for over thirty years. He thrived
on controversy, and his radical politics twice landed him in
jail. One jury condemned him as 'a wicked, malicious and
seditious person who has attempted to stir up discontent
among his Majesty's subjects'.

He refused advertisements for state lotteries,
calling them 'a national nuisance'. He championed
unpopular causes which later became respectable: the anti-
slavery campaign, help for boy chimney-sweeps, overseas
missions and the Bible Society.

Montgomery was expelled from one school for
spending all day writing poetry. When he became famous,
a friend asked which of his poems would last. He replied,
'None, sir, nothing – except perhaps a few of my hymns.'

1

Angels from the realms of glory
Wing your flight o'er all the earth;
Ye who sang creation's story
Now proclaim Messiah's birth:
 Come and worship,
 Worship Christ, the new-born King.

2

Shepherds in the fields abiding,
Watching o'er your flocks by night,
God with man is now residing,
Yonder shines the infant Light:

3

Sages, leave your contemplations,
Brighter visions beam afar;
Seek the great Desire of Nations:
Ye have seen his natal star:

4

Saints before the altar bending,
Watching long in hope and fear,
Suddenly the Lord, descending,
In his temple shall appear:

5

Though an infant now we view him,
He shall fill his Father's throne,
Gather all the nations to him;
Every knee shall then bow down.

JAMES MONTGOMERY (1771–1854)

GIRLS AND BOYS,
LEAVE YOUR TOYS

For many years Sir Malcolm Sargent conducted carol concerts, as well as the Henry Wood Promenade Concerts, at London's Royal Albert Hall. With the added bait of TV cameras from 1953, he took the 'Last Night of the Proms' to a peak of exuberance; the audience cheered and stamped more than ever with their banners, whistles, streamers and balloons. 'Now give your toys back to Nanny!' he admonished on one occasion. He loved it all, earning the nickname 'Flash Harry' for his showmanship.

With all his distinction as a musical ambassador, knighted in 1947, he was a child at heart. He shone early as organist and composer; later he promoted and conducted children's concerts, and after his death in 1967 a Malcolm Sargent Cancer Fund for Children was opened.

So the invitation in this text for the traditional Czech 'Zither Carol' is to girls and boys – of all ages.

1

Girls and boys, leave your toys, make no noise,
    Kneel at his crib and worship him:
At thy shrine, Child divine, we are thine,
    Our Saviour's here!

       Alleluia, the church bells ring;
       Alleluia, the angels sing;
       Alleluia, from everything —
       All must draw near.

2

Shepherds came at the fame of thy name,
    Angels their guide to Bethlehem;
In that place saw thy face filled with grace,
    Stood at thy door.

3

Wise men too haste to do homage new,
    Gold, myrrh and frankincense they bring;
As 'twas said, starlight led to thy bed —
    Bending their knee.

4

O that we all might be good as he,
    Spotless, with God in unity;
Saviour dear, ever near, with us here
    since life began.

HAROLD MALCOLM WATTS SARGENT (1895–1967)

GO, TELL IT
ON THE MOUNTAIN

Nashville, Tennessee, is 'Music City', the world-famous home of country music complete with museum, folk-heroes and souvenirs, and a galaxy of radio stations to match. A century ago it was home for the infant Fisk University's 'Jubilee Singers', whose original members came from the unique generation of freed southern slaves and slaves' children. They took their name from the year of freedom in the Bible.

Most of the two dozen singers were in their twenties; all had already endured much oppression, the traumas of separation from their families, or physical cruelty. Even when free, they suffered more indignity on their singing tours. They were shut out or thrown out of hotels, railway waiting-rooms and ships' cabins because they were black. They met problems in some churches, yet through some highly stressful travels they triumphed by their prayers and their music.

Coming to England, they sang before Gladstone and Queen Victoria. The Prince of Wales, later King Edward VII, thumbed through the pages of their songbook and asked for 'No more auction-block for me', while the Prime Minister's wife picked out 'John Brown's body'. 'Steal away to Jesus' proved a favourite at D. L. Moody's crusade meetings, and at Spurgeon's Tabernacle at his request they sang 'O brothers, don't stay away, for my Lord says there's room enough in the heavens for you'.

This carol is one of many that John Wesley Work Jnr added to their later repertoire. A Nashville-born scholar, he lived and died there; what time he could spare from teaching Latin and Greek at university was given to collecting, arranging and promoting black spirituals.

Go, tell it on the mountain,
Over the hills and everywhere,
Go, tell it on the mountain
That Jesus Christ is born,

1

While shepherds kept their watching
O'er silent flocks by night,
Behold, throughout the heavens
There shone a holy light.

2

The shepherds feared and trembled
When lo! above the earth
Rang out the angel chorus
That hailed our Saviour's birth.

3

And lo! when they had seen it
They all bowed down and prayed;
They travelled on together
To where the babe was laid.

4

Down in a lowly manger
The humble Christ was born
And God sent us salvation
That blessed Christmas morn.

TRADITIONAL AFRO-AMERICAN (19th century)
adapted by JOHN WESLEY WORK JNR (1872–1925)

GOD REST YOU MERRY, GENTLEMEN

Here is a dancing tune that London can claim for its own, having sung it through the streets for perhaps 300 years. Carol-singing may have changed in our lifetime, but where keen little groups still trudge through the snow with torches and music, keeping log fires and mince pies in their minds, this remains a favourite.

Its theme takes us well out of London and into the shires. The opening line, meaning 'God keep you merry', suggests the rural peasantry who have been invited by the lord of the manor to his festivities. The villagers enter the big house and greet the gentry at high table with this rousing and comforting song.

But it is also a narrative carol telling the familiar story in its own way. To some, the Saviour will first bring discomfort; he was born a peasant rather than a gentleman.

1

God rest you merry, gentlemen,
Let nothing you dismay,
For Jesus Christ our Saviour
Was born upon this day
To save us all from Satan's power
When we were gone astray:
O tidings of comfort and joy, comfort and joy,
O tidings of comfort and joy.

2

At Bethlehem in Judah
This holy babe was born,
And laid within a manger
Upon this blessed morn;
At which his mother Mary
Did neither fear nor scorn:

From God our heavenly Father
A heavenly angel came
And unto certain shepherds
Brought tidings of the same
How that in Bethlehem was born
The Son of God by name:

4

'Fear not' then said the angel,
'Let nothing you affright;
This day is born a Saviour
Of a pure virgin bright,
To free all those who trust in him
From Satan's power and might':

5

The shepherds at those tidings
Rejoiced much in mind,
And left their flocks a-feeding
In tempest, storm and wind,
And went to Bethlehem straightway
This blessed babe to find:

6

And when to Bethlehem they came
Whereat this infant lay,
They found him in a manger
Where oxen fed on hay;
His mother Mary, kneeling,
Unto the Lord did pray:

7

Now to the Lord sing praises,
All you within this place,
And with true love and fellowship
Each other now embrace:
This holy tide of Christmas
All anger should efface:

TRADITIONAL (18th century)

31

See Amid The Winter's Snow

1851 when this text appeared was the year of the Great Exhibition at the original Crystal Palace in London's Hyde Park. The winter before had been freezing cold with heavy snow.

After the death of his wife, Edward Caswall had moved to Birmingham and this was one of the first of many hymns he wrote there. He was by now a Roman Catholic; the Anglican John Goss provided a tune which has become wedded to these words. He was organist of St Paul's Cathedral and also composer of the famous tune for 'Praise, my soul, the King of heaven'.

Words and music combine perfectly here; so do two of the Gospels. We sing what Luke tells us of the shepherds, and what John tells us of Jesus, the Lamb of God.

See amid the winter's snow,
Born for us on earth below,
See, the tender Lamb appears,
Promised from eternal years!
Hail, thou ever-blessed morn!
Hail, redemption's happy dawn!
Sing through all Jerusalem:
Christ is born in Bethlehem!

2

Lo, within a manger lies
He who built the starry skies;
He who, throned in height sublime,
Sits amid the cherubim!

3

Say, ye holy shepherds, say,
What your joyful news today?
Wherefore have ye left your sheep
On the lonely mountain steep?

4

'As we watched at dead of night,
Lo, we saw a wondrous light;
Angels singing peace on earth
Told us of a Saviour's birth.'

5

Sacred infant, all-divine,
What a tender love was thine
Thus to come from highest bliss
Down to such a world as this!

6

Teach, O teach us, holy child
by thy face so meek and mild,
Teach us to resemble thee
In thy sweet humility.

EDWARD CASWALL (1814–78)

THE VIRGIN MARY HAD A BABY BOY

James Bryce was born around 1850. Ninety-two years later, as he sang this Caribbean spiritual, fellow West Indian Edric Connor noted down the words and music. Connor published it in his own collection in 1945, and from the 1960s it took off as a very popular Christmas song in the calypso style.

Schools have taken to it well, even where the children sing about 'the verger Mary . . .'! In these days we sometimes have to tell from the beginning the story of Jesus, so that East and West can share the wonder of the child born of a virgin and the glorious kingdom open to believers.

1

The virgin Mary had a baby boy,
The virgin Mary had a baby boy,
The virgin Mary had a baby boy
And they say that his name is Jesus.
He come from the glory,
He come from the glorious kingdom:
He come from the glory,
He come from the glorious kingdom.
O yes, believer! O yes, believer!
He come from the glory,
He come from the glorious kingdom.

2

The angels sang when the baby was born . . .
And they say that his name is Jesus.

3

The shepherds saw where the baby was born . . .
And they say that his name is Jesus.

4

The wise men came when the baby was born . . .
And they say that his name is Jesus.

TRADITIONAL WEST INDIAN

WHILE SHEPHERDS WATCHED
THEIR FLOCKS BY NIGHT

Nahum Tate was a Dublin-born Irishman who became the sixth Poet Laureate of England. He was not universally popular; he wrote and adapted the works of others for the London stage, and was attacked for his pains by Alexander Pope and fellow-Irishman Jonathan Swift.

But until Robert Bridges in the twentieth century, Tate was the only Laureate to write an enduring hymn. This one, published in 1700 in a supplement to the *New Version* of the Psalms, was one of the first to be allowed officially in church services.

He was appointed historiographer-royal; but his character and his career declined together, and he died at Southwark in a refuge for debtors. This single hymn could have made his fortune; as it is, we are still gratefully using the treasure he has bequeathed to us.

1

While shepherds watched
   their flocks by night,
All seated on the ground,
The angel of the Lord came down
And glory shone around.

2

'Fear not' said he (for mighty dread
Had seized their troubled mind);
'Glad tidings of great joy I bring
To you and all mankind:

3

'To you in David's town this day
Is born of David's line
A Saviour, who is Christ the Lord;
And this shall be the sign:

4

'The heavenly babe
  you there shall find
To human view displayed,
All meanly wrapped in swathing bands
And in a manger laid.'

5

Thus spake the seraph, and forthwith
Appeared a shining throng
Of angels praising God, who thus
Addressed their joyful song:

6

'All glory be to God on high
And to the earth be peace:
Good-will henceforth from heaven to men
Begin and never cease'.

NAHUM TATE (1652–1715)

A GREAT
AND MIGHTY WONDER

Istanbul is dominated today by the magnificent sixth-century dome of 'Santa Sophia' (Holy Wisdom). It is one of the greatest triumphs of Byzantine architecture, adapted for use as a mosque and a museum but built as the cathedral of what was then Constantinople — previously Byzantium.

This was the birthplace of the Greek poem by its former patriarch and scholar Germanus, which John Mason Neale rendered into this English hymn.

Neale felt that British Christians were slow to appreciate the treasures of eastern Christianity. In translating Greek hymns he said 'I have had no predecessors, and therefore could have no master'. He kept most of his versions for 'the nine years recommended by Horace' before publishing them; this is one of many to have stood up well in its new language. The Turkish mountains, the blue waters by which Byzantium was built and those who live there today are all invited to join the doxology.

1

A great and mighty wonder,
A full and holy cure!
The virgin bears the infant
with virgin-honour pure:
Repeat the hymn again!
'To God on high be glory
And peace on earth to men.'

2

The Word becomes incarnate
And yet remains on high;
And cherubim sing anthems
To shepherds from the sky:

3

While thus they sing your Monarch,
Those bright angelic bands,
Rejoice, ye vales and mountains,
Ye oceans, clap your hands:

4

Since all he comes to ransom,
By all be Christ adored;
The infant born in Bethl'em,
The Saviour and the Lord:

GERMANUS (about 634–732)

translated by JOHN MASON NEALE (1816–66) and others

DING DONG!
MERRILY ON HIGH

Church bells, said Dorothy L. Sayers, give the loudest noise that is made to the glory of God. George Woodward enjoyed their sound as he ministered in London and East Anglian churches. He kept bees and loved cricket, never missing the annual Eton v. Harrow match at Lords; if Harrow won, so much the better. But his abiding passion was music.

He was a stickler for accuracy and a lover of the antique. He refused to apologize for the 'old-world ring' of his *Cowley Carol Book*, saying it was only fitting 'that the words should be in keeping with the somewhat antiquated tunes whereto they have here been wedded'. This meticulous, sometimes lonely, scholar gave us two of the merriest festival songs, instantly recognizable favourites still.

For Easter he wrote 'This joyful Eastertide'; for Christmas, he used a French dance tune with high two-footed jumps — literally 'kitchen brawls' — to pay this tribute to the bellringers.

1

Ding dong! merrily on high
In heaven the bells are ringing
Ding dong! verily the sky
Is riven with angels singing:
Gloria, Hosanna in excelsis!

2

E'en so here below, below,
Let steeple bells be swungen,
And i-o, i-o, i-o,
By priest and people sungen:

3

Pray you, dutifully prime
Your matin chime, ye ringers;
May you beautifully rhyme
Your evetime song, ye singers:

GEORGE RATCLIFFE WOODWARD (1848–1934)

FROM HEAVEN HIGH
I COME TO EARTH

When in 1535 this carol was first printed at Wittenberg, William Tyndale had just been arrested for translating the Bible, and the first English Prayer Book was still some years ahead. In Germany, Luther's reformation was in full song.

A miner's son and former monk, Martin Luther had also put the Bible into his own language. He was a strong singer who played the lute and flute, setting gospel truth to music in many hymns.

He also loved his brave wife Katherine, who was sometimes 'my rib' but often 'my lord', and their six children — though he did once cut up a pair of Hans' trousers to mend his own with! To another he once exclaimed, 'Child, what have you done that I should love you so? You have disturbed the whole household with your bawling!'

These seven verses are from the fifteen composed for their family Christmas, a 'nativity play in song'. Eight-year-old Hans could have sung the opening lines, taking the angel's part, with the younger children and guests all coming in on cue. Perhaps the new-born baby held the centre of the stage.

One of Luther's students commented on another Christmas in their home, that the now famous doctor was very happy, talking and singing of the incarnation, of God coming among us.

'Oh, we poor men!' he said, 'that we should be so cold and indifferent to this great joy that has been given us. This indeed is the greatest gift, which far exceeds all else that God has created. And we believe so feebly even though the angels proclaim and preach and sing, and their song is fair and sums up the whole Christian religion, for "Glory to God in the highest" is the very heart of worship.'

Roland Bainton, who wrote a biography of Luther, has also translated his family carol.

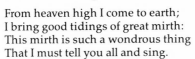

1

From heaven high I come to earth;
I bring good tidings of great mirth:
This mirth is such a wondrous thing
That I must tell you all and sing.

2

A little child for you this morn
Has from a chosen maid been born,
A little child so tender, sweet,
That you should skip upon your feet.

3

How glad we'll be that this is so!
With all the shepherds let us go
To see what God for us has done
In sending us his own dear Son.

4

Look, look, my heart, and let me peek:
Whom in the manger do you seek?
Who is that lovely little one?
The baby Jesus, God's own Son.

5

Be welcome, Lord! Be now our guest:
By you poor sinners have been blessed,
In nakedness and cold you lie:
How can I thank you; how can I?

6

You wanted so to make me know
That you had let all great things go;
You had a palace in the sky:
You left it there for such as I.

7

And if the world were twice as wide,
With gold and precious jewels inside,
Still such a cradle would not do
To hold a babe so great as you.

MARTIN LUTHER (1483–1546)
translated by ROLAND H. BAINTON (1894–1984)

INFANT HOLY

Here is a teasing mixture of known and unknown.

Only in the past sixty years have these English words become established among carols. Edith Reed was a Londoner from Islington whose life's work lay in music for children. She aimed to see and hear songs and hymns through a child's eyes and ears, and published this translation in her own teaching magazine in the 1920s.

But the original carol tune may be ten times the age of the words we know; fourteenth century or earlier. It certainly comes from Poland, but beyond that little is known.

The cattle, it says, did not recognize Jesus in the manger. Some carols suggest that they did; here is another unknown! The 'tidings of a gospel true' are more trustworthy.

1

Infant holy,
Infant lowly,
For his bed a cattle stall;
Oxen lowing,
Little knowing
Christ the babe is Lord of all.
Swift are winging
Angels singing,
Nowells ringing,
Tidings bringing:
  Christ the babe is Lord of all,
  Christ the babe is Lord of all.

2

Flocks were sleeping,
Shepherds keeping
Vigil till the morning new
Saw the glory,
Heard the story,
Tidings of a gospel true.
Thus rejoicing,
Free from sorrow,
Praises voicing
Greet the morrow:
  Christ the babe was born for you,
  Christ the babe was born for you.

ANON. (POLISH)

translated by EDITH MARGARET GELLIBRAND REED (1885–1933)

MARY HAD A BABY

The tiny but mountainous mid-Atlantic island of St Helena, between southern Africa and South America, is famous in history as the last home of the exiled emperor Napoleon. He died there in 1821.

St Helena is also the birthplace of this spiritual which can claim kinship with the many songs coming to Europe and the world from the West Indies. Schools and junior groups have welcomed it, as the tiniest children can join in its simple refrain.

In question-and-answer style, the leader or choir tells the story of the birth of a Saviour for all the world. The emperor is dead: long live the King!

1

Mary had a baby,
Yes, Lord:
Mary had a baby,
Yes, my Lord.
Mary had a baby,
Yes, Lord.
The people keep a-comin'
And the train done gone.

2

What did she name him?
Yes, Lord . . .

3

Mary named him Jesus,
Yes, Lord . . .

4

Where was he born?
Yes, Lord . . .

5

Born in a stable,
Yes, Lord . . .

6

Where did she lay him?
Yes, Lord . . .

7

Laid him in a manger,
Yes, Lord . . .

TRADITIONAL ST HELENA

REJOICE AND BE MERRY

' "If you'll thrive in musical religion, stick to strings," says I. "Strings be safe soul-lifters, as far as that do go," said Mr Spinks.'

Dewy, Mail, Penny, Spinks, Bowman and Leaf comprise the Mellstock parish quire, or church orchestra, who meet on Christmas Eve in Thomas Hardy's *Under the Greenwood Tree*. Written in Dorchester, this novel established Hardy's literary reputation.

He nearly called it *The Mellstock Quire*. His father and grandfather had both played in such a band; the old carol books and the music of fiddle, bass viol, serpent and clarinet spoke of their Dorset heritage which was already changing.

The 'quires' would have played and sung just such a carol as this from an old Dorset church-gallery book. After a century and a half of domination by organs, other church musicians are today coming into their own again. Like the first gifts offered to Christ, our praises show his glory.

1   Rejoice and be merry in songs and in mirth:
    O praise our Redeemer, all mortals on earth!
    For this is the birthday of Jesus our King
    Who brought us salvation – his praises we'll sing.

    2   A heavenly vision appeared in the sky;
        Vast numbers of angels the shepherds did spy
        Proclaiming the birthday of Jesus our King
        Who brought us salvation — his praises we'll sing.

3   Likewise a bright star in the sky did appear,
    Which led the wise men from the east to draw near;
    They found the Messiah, sweet Jesus our King
    who brought us salvation — his praises we'll sing.

    4   And when they were come, they their treasures unfold,
        And unto him offer myrrh, incense and gold:
        So blessed for ever be Jesus our King
        Who brought us salvation — his praises we'll sing.

DORSET CHURCH-GALLERY BOOK

SHEPHERDS CAME

The shepherds, says George Caird, were despised by the orthodox because the nature of their job made religious observance haphazard. But they were Christ's first worshippers — forerunners of the ordinary people who later heard him gladly. 'The wonder with which the shepherds' story was greeted prepares us for the deeper wonder to come.'

Dr Caird wrote this in his *Pelican Gospel Commentary* on St Luke; twenty years before, he had made this English translation of an early Latin carol on the 'pastores' — the shepherds.

A Scotsman who worked in Canada and Oxford, the writer was a brilliant classical scholar and a skilled Bible teacher. He was born near the end of the First World War and wrote this near the end of the Second; he was known as a man of peace, discovering like the shepherds where true peace is found.

1

Shepherds came, their praises bringing,
Who had heard the angels singing
'Far from you be fear unruly,
Christ is King of glory born.'

2

Wise men whom a star had guided
Incense, gold and myrrh provided,
Made their sacrifices truly
To the King of glory born.

3

Jesus, born the King of heaven,
Christ to us through Mary given,
To your praise and honour duly
Be resounding glory done.

LATIN (15th century)
translated by GEORGE BRADFORD CAIRD (1917–84)

BRIGHTEST AND BEST
OF THE SONS OF THE MORNING

Watching for scorpions while travelling in India, Bishop Heber once found he had eye contact with a snake which had slid on to his shoulder. He lived to thank God it didn't bite him.

Most animal and plant life delighted him; among riverside palms, fireflies and nightingales, evening flowers and music, he wrote, 'I feel in my heart it is good to be here.' But human cruelty and degradation distressed him, and constant travel by horse or elephant in intense heat cut short his life in the East.

Whether versifying 'Bluebeard' for family parties or making poetry which helped to get hymns formally approved among Anglicans, his writing is full of music and colour. His journal records one Indian journey when he heard this hymn (for which he preferred the tune 'Wandering Willie') sung 'better than I ever heard in a church before'. He can hardly have known when he wrote it how far east he would travel and his words would be sung.

1　Brightest and best of the sons of the morning,
　　Dawn on our darkness and lend us thine aid:
　　Star of the east, the horizon adorning,
　　Guide where our infant Redeemer is laid.

　　　　2　Cold on his cradle the dewdrops are shining,
　　　　　　Low lies his head with the beasts of the stall;
　　　　　　Angels adore him in slumber reclining,
　　　　　　Maker and Monarch and Saviour of all.

3　Say, shall we yield him, in costly devotion,
　　Odours of Edom and offerings divine?
　　Gems of the mountain and pearls of the ocean,
　　Myrrh from the forest or gold from the mine?

　　　　4　Vainly we offer each ample oblation,
　　　　　　Vainly with gifts would his favour secure;
　　　　　　Richer by far is the heart's adoration,
　　　　　　Dearer to God are the prayers of the poor.

REGINALD HEBER (1783–1826)

CHRIST THE WORLD'S
LIGHT NOW IS WAKING

One day in 1987, Keith Landis was working in the study of his California rectory in a suburb of Los Angeles. Suddenly he heard shouts from the hallway: 'Hey, is anybody home? Your house is on fire!'

Flames were leaping out of another room and had been spotted by a neighbour before the rector knew what was happening. He raced out of the door but then had second thoughts. Running back to the study, he gathered up all he could from years of research and writing about hymns and hymnody. Some items were lost, and three rooms of his single-storey house were gutted; but he had succeeded in rescuing many precious files and notebooks.

Another crateload of books was lost somewhere across the Atlantic. But Keith presses on, writing words and music as well as studying and collecting the work of others. This hymn which survived the blaze was composed the year before, to celebrate the Epiphany and provide a joyful opening act of praise. Here is the Light that comes not to destroy but to save.

1

> Christ the world's Light now is waking,
> Glory from his throne-room breaking!
> Light of Light, no longer hidden
> Holds high court for kings star-bidden.
> *Alleluia! Alleluia!*

2

> Glorious day of revelation!
> Face to face with incarnation,
> Gentiles worship, awe-struck, kneeling,
> Godhead seeing, hearing, feeling!
> *Alleluia! Alleluia!*

3

Offer they in fullest measure
Homage for their High King's pleasure,
Precious gifts, all prophesying
God's own Son for sinners dying!
Alleluia! Alleluia!

4

Now he comes to us gift-bearing,
Riches of the Spirit sharing!
With your bounty, Lord, astound us!
Through us light the world around us!
Alleluia! Alleluia!

KEITH LANDIS (born 1922)

EARTH HAS MANY A NOBLE CITY

Both the English translator and the original author of this hymn had two distinct parts to their lives.

Edward Caswall, the son of a country vicar, was himself ordained. In his thirties he became a Roman Catholic, joining John Henry Newman at Birmingham; part of the scholarly work to which he then gave himself was the translation of over 200 Latin hymns. This is one of many enjoyed by all kinds of Christians.

The fourth century Spanish judge Prudentius rose to be chief of the imperial bodyguard. But when at fifty-six he started writing his memoirs he was deeply ashamed of what he now saw as a sinful and worldly life. He dedicated himself to God and during his last ten years wrote several hymns. This one is marked for use at Epiphany.

1

Earth has many a noble city;
Bethl'em, thou dost all excel!
Out of thee the Lord from heaven
Came to rule his Israel.

2

Fairer than the sun at morning
Was the star that told his birth,
To the world its God announcing,
Seen in fleshly form on earth.

3

Eastern sages at his cradle
Make oblations rich and rare;
See them give, in deep devotion,
Gold and frankincense and myrrh.

4

Sacred gifts of mystic meaning:
Incense doth their God disclose;
Gold the King of kings proclaimeth;
Myrrh his sepulchre foreshows.

5

Jesus whom the Gentiles worshipped,
At thy glad Epiphany,
Unto thee, with God the Father
And the Spirit, glory be!

AURELIUS CLEMENS PRUDENTIUS (348–about 410)
translated by EDWARD CASWALL (1814–78) and others

LULLAY LULLAY,
THOU LITTLE TINY CHILD

At the south-west corner of Coventry Cathedral stands a large wooden cross; on the wall behind it are the words 'Father, forgive'. The cross was made from two charred beams which fell from the roof of the fifteenth-century building destroyed by aerial bombing in November 1940. The words were chosen as a reminder that after slaughter and wreckage in many cities, it is not only 'the enemy' who needs forgiveness.

This exquisite but almost heart-rending carol was sung at Coventry in the early days of that former place of worship; the text goes back at least as far as 1534. It has painful links with the cruelties of our own century.

The 'Coventry Carol' was part of the medieval mystery-play performed by the local craft guilds in that Midland city, which the motor industry has made prosperous in recent times. When work and faith were seen as one, the people acted out the pain and the joy of the Christmas story.

Following the narrative of the Gospel according to Matthew, these verses are sung by the women of Bethlehem. Immediately afterwards, Herod's soldiers rush in to slay their children, in a vain effort to get rid of the new King.

Even on Christ's birthday, sorrow is not far away. Part of our response to him is humble heart-searching.

Lullay lullay, thou little tiny child,
  By by, lullay lullay:
Lullay, lullay, thou little tiny child,
  By by, lullay lullay.

1

O sisters too,
How may we do
  For to preserve this day
This poor youngling,
For whom we sing
  By by, lullay lullay?

2

Herod the king
In his raging
  Charged he hath this day
His men of might
In his own sight
  All children young to slay.

3

That woe is me,
Poor child, for thee,
  And ever mourn and say,
For thy parting
Neither say nor sing
  By by, lullay lullay.

PAGEANT OF THE GUILD OF SHEARMEN
AND TAILORS (15th century)

THE FIRST NOWELL

This may be the nearest that some choirs and congregations get to singing football songs in church! It bears all the marks of a 'carol' in the original sense of an outdoor dance in the round; the tune is simple and the words in their earliest known form seem to have been made up on the spot. The syllables vary, the story is confused, and one or two bits of nonsense are thrown in.

Some musicians feel the tune must be a descant of a more varied original. The old Cornishman who sang it to the collector William Sandys in 1827 may have been remembering just his own part.

Purists hold to the old text, though that must have been fairly flexible. Recent books have ventured to tidy up some of the words, but the tune is not likely to be supplanted. 'Nowell' itself may be a corruption of *Natalis* for 'Birthday'; on birthdays anything can happen.

1

The first nowell the
   angel did say
Was to certain poor
   shepherds in fields as they lay;
In fields where they lay
   a-keeping their sheep
On a cold winter's night
   that was so deep.
Nowell, nowell, nowell, nowell!
Born is the King of Israel.

2

Wise men looked up
   and saw a star
Shining in the east,
   beyond them far;
And to the earth it
   gave great light,
And so it continued
   both day and night.

3

So by the light of that
   same star
They came with haste
   from country far;
To seek for a king they
   made their way
And they reached the
   place where Jesus lay.

4

Then entered in those
   wise men three
Full reverently upon
   their knee,
And offered there in
   his presence
Their gold and myrrh
   and frankincense.

5

Then let us all with one
   accord
Sing praises to our
   heavenly Lord,
Who hath made heaven
   and earth of nought
And with his blood
   mankind hath bought.

TRADITIONAL (17th century)

WE THREE KINGS

East is east and west is west — and they meet together in this carol from the mid-nineteenth century. It is a song about the east, written in the west by the American John Henry Hopkins Jnr.

The wise men or Magi may not have been kings, but the royal tradition dies hard in the United States! Nor do we know how many there were, let alone the names they are sometimes saddled with.

But no other carol, old or new, gives these eastern sages such direct speech, such dramatic opportunities, or such a rich exploration of the meaning of their gifts.

John Hopkins senior was by turns an industrialist, lawyer and bishop. His son shows in this carol the ear of a musician, the tongue of a journalist and the eye of a stained-glass designer.

1

We three kings of Orient are;
Bearing gifts we traverse afar
Field and fountain,
  moor and mountain,
Following yonder star;

O star of wonder, star of night,
Star with royal beauty bright,
Westward leading, still proceeding,
Guide us to thy perfect light.

2

Born a King on Bethlehem plain,
Gold I bring to crown him again;
King for ever, ceasing never,
Over us all to reign

3

Frankincense to offer have I,
Incense owns a deity nigh;
Prayer and praising, all men raising,
Worship him, God most high.

4

Myrrh is mine; its bitter perfume
Breathes a life of gathering gloom;
Sorrowing, sighing, bleeding, dying
Sealed in the stone-cold tomb:

5

Glorious now behold him arise,
King, and God, and Sacrifice;
Heaven sings 'Alleluia':
'Alleluia', the earth replies:

JOHN HENRY HOPKINS (1820–91)

UNTO US A BOY IS BORN

During the First World War, Percy Dearmer worked as a Red Cross Chaplain; after it, as Professor of Ecclesiastical Art. Earlier, he founded the Christian Social Union; later, he was Librarian of Westminster Abbey. The parishes he served included Chelsea and Camberwell, Marylebone and Mayfair; but it was at Primrose Hill in north London where his gifts for liturgy and music blossomed most fully. While Vicar there he helped edit the *English Hymnal*, and soon afterwards masterminded the very different *Songs of Praise*. Few men have influenced hymn-singing so much.

This is his translation of what he called a 'rollicking Latin text'. Of the inevitable variations in versions he said 'it is the last editor who matters'; of the book where it first appeared, '*Songs of Praise* is for all the churches; not indeed for Lot's wife, but for the forward-looking people of every communion.'

1

Unto us a boy is born!
King of all creation,
Came he to a world forlorn,
The Lord of every nation.

2

Cradled in a stall was he
With sleepy cows and asses;
But the very beasts could see
That he all men surpasses.

3

Herod then with fear was filled;
'A prince,' he said 'in Jewry!'
All the little boys he killed
At Bethl'em in his fury.

4

Now may Mary's son, who came
So long ago to love us,
Lead us all with hearts aflame
Unto the joys above us.

5

Omega and Alpha he!
Let the organ thunder
While the choir with peals of glee
Doth rend the air asunder.

LATIN ANON. (15th century)
translated by PERCY DEARMER (1837–1936)

Born In The Night

Joe and Mary arrived at the Central Line station at Loughton on the London Underground. It was Christmas Eve 1958. Before they got much further, Mary's time was up, and a friendly filling station attendant gave them a little room above the office and went to put the kettle on.

Two bus conductresses coming off duty up the hill met a paper boy whistling 'Angels from the realms of glory'. 'Hey, what a laugh!' he called, 'Have you heard? A girl's just had a baby in the filling station!'

So began the story as acted by the youth club at the local Methodist church, guided by their minister Geoffrey Ainger. A screen beside the actors showed colour slides of the route the holy family took through the local streets. They had some guitars, so he added this song as a finale.

More songs came from his work at Notting Hill, but only after they had sold 13,000 copies did a publisher show any interest! This one is now in many books. After a spell in teaching, and writing *Jesus our Contemporary*, Geoffrey is now back working as a minister in Orpington, Kent. Jesus is still among us; one day all shall see him.

Born in the night, Mary's child,
A long way from your home;
Coming in need, Mary's child,
Born in a borrowed room.

2

Clear shining light, Mary's child,
Your face lights up our way;
Light up our world, Mary's child,
Dawn on our darkened day.

3

Truth of our life, Mary's child,
You tell us God is good;
Prove it is true, Mary's child,
Go to your cross of wood.

4

Hope of the world, Mary's child,
You're coming soon to reign;
King of the earth, Mary's child,
Walk in our streets again.

GEOFFREY AINGER (born 1925)

CHRISTIANS, AWAKE!

When Dr Byrom asked his daughter Dorothy what she would like for Christmas, this unusual teenager said 'Please write me a poem.' So the original double page where the hymn was first written is headed 'Christmas Day, for Dolly'. It was reputedly waiting for her on the breakfast table on Christmas morning 1749 — complete with blots and crossings out, as if daddy had struggled with it late into the night!

Other hands have crossed out or changed more of the words since then, but the Christmas present has lasted well. In 1750 the Byrom household were treated to a rendering of it at their door, by 'the singing men and boys with Mr Wainwright'. John Wainwright was the new organist at Stockport Parish Church where it then had its first airing, to the tune he had composed and to which we still sing it.

John Byrom was the son of a Manchester draper; he was so tall that he found it hard to find a horse big enough for him to ride. He carried a stick with a crook top, and his friendly, inquisitive face peered out from under the wide brim of a curious slouched hat. He trained in literature at Cambridge and medicine in France, but his other main claim to fame is in pioneering his own system of shorthand.

At first he divulged his secret to only a few, including Gibbon, Horace Walpole and Lord Chesterfield; later he lived mainly by teaching it. He was a friend of the Wesley brothers who both adopted the system since the day in 1736 when Charles refused to correspond further with John unless by the Byrom method.

1

Christians, awake! salute the happy morn
Whereon the Saviour of the world was born;
Rise to adore the mystery of love
Which hosts of angels chanted from above;
With them the joyful tidings first begun
Of God incarnate and the virgin's Son.

2

Then to the watchful shepherds it was told,
Who heard the angelic herald's voice, 'Behold,
I bring good tidings of a Saviour's birth
To you and all the nations upon earth:
This day hath God fulfilled his promised word,
This day is born a Saviour, Christ the Lord!'

3

He spake; and straightway the celestial choir
In hymns of joy, unknown before, conspire;
The praises of redeeming love they sang
And heaven's whole orb with Alleluias rang:
God's highest glory was their anthem still,
Peace upon earth, and unto men good will.

4

To Bethl'em straight the enlightened shepherds ran
To see the wonder God had wrought for man,
And found, with Joseph and the blessed maid,
Her son, the Saviour, in a manger laid:
Amazed, the wondrous story they proclaim,
The first apostles of his infant fame.

5

O may we keep and ponder in our mind
God's wondrous love in saving lost mankind;
Trace we the babe, who hath retrieved our loss
From his poor manger to his bitter cross:
Tread in his steps, assisted by his grace,
Till man's first heavenly state again takes place.

6

Then may we hope, the angelic hosts among,
To sing, redeemed, a glad triumphal song:
He that was born upon this joyful day
Around us all his glory shall display;
Saved by his love, incessant we shall sing
Eternal praise to heaven's almighty King.

JOHN BYROM (1691–1763)

GOOD CHRISTIANS ALL, REJOICE!

When John Mason Neale was at East Grinstead he helped to revive the dying art of carol-singing. He published books of carols for Christmas and Easter, and led a group of men and boys with lanterns to sing in the village.

Among them was his son Vincent, who remembered how on Christmas Eve 'the chief stand was in the main street and was a picturesque sight, with the glare of the torches, and the players of the string and wind instruments. The baker played the bass fiddle; all formed in a large circle with the singers inside the ring.'

This carol (originally limited to 'Christian *men*'!) was freely adapted by Dr Neale from the very old German-Latin 'In dulci jubilo'. A fourteenth-century mystic said that the words were sung to him by angels, who invited him to join their dance. Certainly the carol is in tune with the message of the heavenly host.

1

Good Christians all, rejoice
With heart and soul and voice!
Give ye heed to what we say:
Jesus Christ is born today.
Ox and ass before him bow
And he is in the manger now:
  Christ is born today,
  Christ is born today.

2

Good Christians all, rejoice
With heart and soul and voice!
Now ye hear of endless bliss;
Jesus Christ was born for this.
He hath oped the heavenly door
And we are blessed for evermore:
  Christ was born for this,
  Christ was born for this.

3

Good Christians all, rejoice
With heart and soul and voice!
Now ye need not fear the grave;
Jesus Christ was born to save,
Calls you one and calls you all
To gain his everlasting hall:
  Christ was born to save,
  Christ was born to save.

GERMAN-LATIN, ANON. (14th century)
translated by JOHN MASON NEALE (1818–66)

HOLY CHILD

'If an author is allowed favourite texts,' says the Bishop of Thetford, 'this is one of mine.' He wrote it at Sevenoaks in Kent soon after the birth of his youngest child.

A lifelong poetry-lover, Timothy Dudley-Smith produced comic verse as a Cambridge student; he calls this 'an invaluable part of learning the trade'. His first hymn, 'Tell out, my soul, the greatness of the Lord', came in 1960 while he was working with the Church Pastoral-Aid Society.

He and his wife Arlette began a custom of including a new hymn-text on their family Christmas card each year; this one appeared in 1966. He generously attributes much of its popularity to the tune written by Michael Baughen and David Wilson three years later.

Timothy was made a bishop in 1981. The Christmas card habit has built up an unequalled range of hymns about the holy child and the reason why he was born.

1

Holy child, how still you lie!
  Safe the manger, soft the hay;
Faint upon the eastern sky
  Breaks the dawn of Christmas
    Day.

2

Holy child, whose birthday brings
  Shepherds from their field and fold,
Angel choirs and eastern kings,
  Myrrh and frankincense and gold:

3

Holy child, what gift of grace
  From the Father freely willed!
In your infant form we trace
  All God's promises fulfilled.

4

Holy child, whose human years
  Span like ours delight and pain;
One in human joys and tears,
  One in all but sin and stain:

5

Holy child, so far from home,
  All the lost to seek and save,
To what dreadful death you come,
  To what dark and silent grave!

6

Holy child, before whose name
  Powers of darkness faint and fall;
Conquered, death and sin and shame —
  Jesus Christ is Lord of all!

7

Holy child, how still you lie!
  Safe the manger, soft the hay;
Clear upon the eastern sky
  Breaks the dawn of Christmas Day.

TIMOTHY DUDLEY-SMITH (born 1926)

SING LULLABY

Whoever pronounced baby Sabine Baring-Gould 'delicate' may have been looking at the wrong child. He lived into his nineties as a romantic and eccentric extrovert of unrivalled energy.

Soon after ordination he married a Yorkshire mill-girl; they had five sons and nine daughters. He inherited a 3,000-acre estate at Lew Trenchard in Devon, and when the rector of the parish died he appointed himself to the job of caring for the 266 souls who lived there, as well as being their squire.

He would send advance notice of a pastoral visit, being driven round by his coachman in a large carriage. Having talked and prayed with the families, he then returned to the Manor library to work standing at his high wooden desk.

In this way he wrote some 160 books, including two pioneer collections of local folk songs and fifteen huge volumes of *Lives of the Saints*. For works on European travel he drew partly on boyhood memories; his novels had exotic titles and his histories tackled Napoleon and the Caesars. He urged the return of sacred dance and drama together with carols for all seasons, to extol the glory of the incarnation.

The English church, he said, was stiff and slow to move, but he saw signs of growing vitality and confidence. Carols could be part of such life — 'not out of church in wind and rain and frost and snow, but within the church, in the midst of light and warmth and colour'.

Not the least marvel of a swashbuckling Victorian churchman was that the same hand and pen gave us 'Widdecombe Fair', 'Onward Christian soldiers', and this most gentle of carols.

1

Sing lullaby!
Lullaby baby, now reclining,
Sing lullaby!
Hush, do not wake the infant King.
Angels are watching, stars are shining
Over the place where he is lying:
Sing lullaby.

2

Sing lullaby!
Lullaby baby, now a-sleeping,
Sing lullaby!
Hush, do not wake the infant King.
Soon will come sorrow with the morning,
Soon will come bitter grief and weeping:
Sing lullaby.

3

Sing lullaby!
Lullaby baby, now a-dozing,
Sing lullaby!
Hush, do not wake the infant King.
Soon comes the cross, the nails, the piercing,
Then in the grave at last reposing:
Sing lullaby.

4

Sing lullaby!
Lullaby! Is the babe awaking?
Sing lullaby!
Hush, do not wake the infant King.
Dreaming of Easter, gladsome morning,
Conquering death, its bondage breaking!
Sing lullaby!

SABINE BARING-GOULD (1834–1924)

SMALL WONDER
THE STAR

Child photography and the writing of verse are two of Paul Wigmore's enthusiasms. He joined a photographic firm at sixteen; later he travelled round the world with top photographers as Art Director for major calendar projects. Recently he has concentrated on portraits, and since taking early retirement has seen his first book of poems in print.

Paul has always enjoyed writing and declaiming light verse; John Betjeman encouraged him to make his work more widely known. His first hymn was published in 1982, and he was working on some Christmas ideas when the phrase 'no small wonder' kept running around his mind.

He made the connection between those three words and Christmas, and this new carol was on the way. It was sung in St Paul's Cathedral at the launch of *Carols for Today* in 1986, to a tune by Paul Edwards who was once a chorister there.

1

Small wonder the star,
    Small wonder the light,
The angels in chorus,
    The shepherds in fright;
But stable and manger for God –
No small wonder!

2

Small wonder the kings,
    Small wonder they bore
The gold and the incense,
    The myrrh, to adore;
But God gives his life on a cross –
No small wonder!

3

Small wonder the love,
    Small wonder the grace,
The power, the glory,
    The light of his face;
But all to redeem my poor heart –
No small wonder!

PAUL WIGMORE (born 1925)

THE HOLLY AND THE IVY

In Chaucer's *Canterbury Tales* the Nun's Priest relates his powerful farmyard melodrama of the cock, the hen and the fox, which the Host acclaims as a merry tale. Of Chanticleer the vain cockerel, he says, 'His voice was merrier than the merry organ'; this was the squeaky portable instrument, small and tough enough for use in processions, celebrated in the familiar carol.

Its colourful word-music reveals a Christian festival adopting all kinds of emblems from religions of earth and evergreen; boys and girls could still dance to its male and female imagery, now consecrated to Christ.

In our own century, song-collector Cecil Sharp re-discovered the carol at Chipping Campden. Gloucestershire and Somerset are its likely homes, and they were certainly singing it in Chaucer's day.

1

The holly and the ivy,
When they are both full-grown,
Of all the trees that are in the wood,
The holly bears the crown.
The rising of the sun
And the running of the deer
The playing of the merry organ,
Sweet singing in the choir.

2

The holly bears a blossom
As white as lily flower,
And Mary bore sweet Jesus Christ
To be our sweet Saviour.

3

The holly bears a berry
As red as any blood,
And Mary bore sweet Jesus Christ
To do poor sinners good.

4

The holly bears a prickle
As sharp as any thorn,
And Mary bore sweet Jesus Christ
On Christmas Day in the morn.

5

The holly bears a bark
As bitter as any gall,
And Mary bore sweet Jesus Christ
For to redeem us all.

TRADITIONAL

AWAY IN A MANGER

Some of the best-known songs and hymns have the least-known origins. When *Dainty songs for little lads and lasses* appeared in Cincinnati in 1887, this children's carol was called 'Luther's Cradle Hymn'. But Martin Luther certainly had nothing to do with it; it has not been traced before 1885, when a Lutheran book from Philadelphia called it 'anonymous'.

So we can say it is American, and that the third verse was added later, linked with the name J. T. MacFarland. The tune 'Cradle Song' is also American, probably travelling to Britain with the Moody and Sankey crusades, and then all around the world.

1

Away in a manger, no crib for a bed,
The little Lord Jesus laid down his sweet head;
The stars in the bright sky looked down where he lay,
The little Lord Jesus asleep on the hay.

2

The cattle are lowing, the baby awakes,
But little Lord Jesus, no crying he makes;
I love thee, Lord Jesus: look down from the sky
And stay by my side until morning is nigh.

3

Be near me, Lord Jesus: I ask thee to stay
Close by me for ever, and love me I pray;
Bless all the dear children in thy tender care
And fit us for heaven, to live with there.

ANON (19th century) Verse 3 JOHN MACFARLAND 1906

ALL MY HEART
THIS NIGHT REJOICES

Albert Schweitzer called Gerhardt 'the king of hymn-writers'; Catherine Winkworth, a queen among translators, said he was the George Herbert of the Lutheran church. If Luther's keynote was faith, Gerhardt's was the love of God. The German and English versions of this hymn are two centuries apart, but this partnership in praise has enriched many Christmases.

Living mostly near her father's Manchester silk business but joining a brilliant circle of distinguished scholars and statesmen, Catherine translated nearly 400 hymns. She relied mainly on German editions of hymnody collected and published by Baron Bunsen, the Prussian ambassador and a family friend of the Winkworths. She spent her final years at Clifton near Bristol pioneering women's education, but was alarmed when a newspaper linked her with the campaign for women's rights.

Paulus Gerhardt was the son of a burgomaster or chief magistrate of a town in Saxony. His early life was clouded with the 'woe and danger' of the Thirty Years' War. A fire started by soldiers destroyed his home, the church building, and many priceless books and papers.

Ordination at 44 and marriage at 48 to his landlord's young daughter Anna Maria led to his happiest years as pastor of a church in Berlin. But only one of their five children survived infancy; he was humiliated by being deposed from office, and with his wife's death after a long illness, his later years were troubled.

The hymns were born out of many trials; their joy in Christ is all the sweeter for it.

All my heart this night rejoices
    As I hear, far and near,
Sweetest angel-voices:
'Christ is born!' their choirs are singing,
    Till the air everywhere
Now with joy is ringing.

2

Hark! a voice from yonder manger,
    Soft and sweet, doth entreat:
'Flee from woe and danger;
People, come; from all doth grieve you
    You are freed; all you need
I will surely give you.'

3

Come then, let us hasten yonder;
    Here let all, great and small,
Kneel in awe and wonder;
Love him who with love is yearning;
    Hail the star that from far
Bright with hope is burning.

4

Thee, O Lord, with love I'll cherish,
    Live to thee, and with thee
Dying, shall not perish,
But shall dwell with thee for ever
    Far on high in the joy
That can alter never.

PAULUS GERHARDT (1607–76)
translated by CATHERINE WINKWORTH (1827–78)

COME AND BE
SURPRISED,
ALL NATIONS

Born at Haarlem in Holland, Fred Kaan lived as a teenager through the Nazi occupation. For two years his parents sheltered a Jewish woman in their home, and later an escaped political prisoner. Three grandparents perished from hunger in the last winter of the war; his mother very nearly succumbed, and his wife's missionary father died in a far-eastern prison camp.

Giving up plans to go to art school, Fred came to England and in 1961 became minister of Plymouth's 'Pilgrim Church': 'in this church,' they said, 'everything is possible!' This was one of the first hymns he wrote there, beginning with an echo of a Dutch carol.

Fred's work has taken him to over sixty different countries; he loves jazz, the history of words, and 'the risk and excitement of ad hoc discipleship'. He remains committed to the cause of the oppressed, to peace, and to God, who still calls all nations.

1

Come and be surprised, all nations,
Here behold the love divine;
Love to still all aspirations,
God concerned with humankind.
Come and see this speechless speaking,
See the Word in human form;
Love through every barrier breaking,
Love as basis, end and norm.

2

Come and see how Jesus entered
Earthly life, as did we all;
See how kings and workers centred
Round this baby in a stall.
See him, who in splendour great is,
For a time in homely care,
See how Christ in humble status
Came with us our life to share.

3

To your holy invitation
We respond, and come, and see;
Kindle our imagination
That our joys may lasting be.
Jesus, by your caring save us,
By your passion heal our pain;
Let no fear nor death enslave us:
By your Easter may we reign!

FREDERIK HERMAN KAAN (born 1929)

HOW DARK WAS THE NIGHT OF HIS COMING

Fred Pratt Green worked in his father's Liverpool leather business before becoming a Methodist minister. Two special friends helped to develop his writing talent.

He met Fallon Webb, who was crippled with severe arthritis, on a chance pastoral visit. They discovered a shared love of poetry and for nearly twenty years kept up a friendship of mutual criticism and encouragement of each other's work.

Later, teacher and musician John Wilson provided similar impetus to his hymn-writing, which flowered so fully after his official retirement that no Methodist since the Wesleys has given us such hymns as Fred has.

This carol, 'a vision of angels', is based on a Welsh text and sung to a Welsh tune — a hint of the author's schooldays in Wales. It sings of the wind; Fred once said of his Christian faith, 'Though the winds of change have disturbed my roots a little, I have never felt uprooted.'

1

How dark was the night of his coming!
How bleak was the wind on the hill!
How many, who slept till cock-crowing,
Had little to wake for but ill!
Good shepherds, who stare into heaven,
What see you so fair and so rare?
What glory transfigures your faces?
What songs are enchanting the air?

2

Those dutiful shepherds saw angels
Where most of us only see night;
Their beautiful vision escapes us
Who cease to believe in the light.
The song is tossed back into darkness
By winds that are bitter with hate;
But shepherds have found in a manger
That Saviour the ages await.

3

You angels, we see you, we hear you!
We stand with our backs to the wind!
The longer we listen, the stronger
Your message of hope for mankind.
You sceptics and cynics, forgive us
For leaving you out in the cold;
We'll come back with songs of salvation,
Good news that shall never grow old.

FREDERICK PRATT GREEN (born 1903)

IN THE
BLEAK MID-WINTER

Christina Rossetti came from an exceptional family. Her father was an Italian patriot and refugee who became a professor at King's College London, and her brothers were cultural leaders of a new movement in the arts.

She was described as 'strikingly beautiful', and as well as teaching she sat as a painter's model for Millais, Holman Hunt, and her brother Dante Gabriel Rossetti. She formed deep attachments but rejected two proposals of marriage from suitors who did not share her Christian and Anglican faith.

She became a notable writer of verse such as *Goblin Market* and prose such as *The Face of the Deep*, a devotional commentary on the Book of Revelation. One of the few hymn-writers with an honoured place among poets, she is well represented in major poetry collections. Because she suffered both physical pain and emotional disappointment, some of her verse is sombre and melancholy.

These happier lines were written as a poem, but ever since *The English Hymnal* published them, with Gustav Holst's tune, in 1906, few carol books have been able to ignore them. The snow may be poetic licence in the Christmas story; for the writer, the believing heart is the only conceivable response.

1

In the bleak mid-winter
  Frosty wind made moan,
Earth stood hard as iron,
  Water like a stone;
Snow had fallen, snow on snow,
  Snow on snow,
In the bleak mid-winter
  Long ago.

2

Our God, heaven cannot hold him,
  Nor earth sustain;
Heaven and earth shall flee away
  When he comes to reign:
In the bleak mid-winter
  A stable place sufficed
The Lord God almighty,
  Jesus Christ.

3

Enough for him, whom cherubim
  Worship night and day,
A breastful of milk
  And a mangerful of hay;
Enough for him, whom angels
  Fall down before,
The ox and ass and camel
  Which adore.

4

Angels and archangels
  May have gathered there,
Cherubim and seraphim
  Thronged the air;
But only his mother
  In her maiden bliss
Worshipped the Beloved
  With a kiss.

5

What can I give him,
  Poor as I am?
If I were a shepherd
  I would bring a lamb;
If I were a wise man
  I would do my part;
Yet what I can I give him —
  Give my heart.

CHRISTINA GEORGINA ROSSETTI (1830–94)

SEE HIM LYING
ON A BED OF STRAW

Not many carols find their way on to postage stamps. But such was the Caribbean flavour of this 'Calypso Carol' that Nevis and the Leeward Islands featured it on theirs for Christmas 1983, printed on each of four different stamps. It has been published in the Bahamas, and sung all over the world in German, Swedish, Welsh and English.

But both words and music come from London! Michael Perry wrote them for a carol service when a student at Oak Hill College; he was stirred when a preacher asked 'How would you like to be born in a cowshed?'

A prolific writer, editor and translator, Michael is now a country vicar; in his Hampshire garden live many animals including Bossy the donkey, who would have felt at home in the stable, straw bed and all.

1   See him lying on a bed of straw.
    A draughty stable with an open door;
    Mary cradling the babe she bore —
    The Prince of glory is his name.
    O now carry me to Bethlehem
    To see the Lord appear to men;
    Just as poor as was the stable then,
    The Prince of glory when he came.

2   Star of silver, sweep across the skies,
    Show where Jesus in the manger lies;
    Shepherds, swiftly from your stupor rise
    To see the Saviour of the world!

3   Angels, sing again the song you sang,
    Bring God's glory to the heart of man;
    Sing that Bethl'em's little baby can
    Be salvation to the soul.

4   Mine are riches, from your poverty;
    From your innocence, eternity;
    Mine, forgiveness by your death for me,
    Child of sorrow for my joy.

MICHAEL ARNOLD PERRY (born 1942)

O LITTLE TOWN
OF BETHLEHEM

The writer of this hymn was pronounced 'a conspicuous failure' as a young teacher. But things were different when he trained for the ministry of the church and was ordained. He became one of the outstanding pastors and preachers of his day, and taught many students with his definition of Christian preaching as 'Truth through Personality'.

Six foot six and single, Phillips Brooks was made a bishop in the American Episcopal Church. He often quoted hymns in his sermons; as a boy he had committed over 200 to memory.

This was written for his Sunday school, inspired by an unforgettable visit to the Holy Land. Christmas 1866 found him in Bethlehem; that town, he knew, could also make its mark on many 'who have not seen, and yet believe'.

O little town of Bethlehem,
How still we see thee lie!
Above thy deep and dreamless
sleep
The silent stars go by:
Yet in thy dark streets shineth
The everlasting Light;
The hopes and fears of all
the years
Are met in thee tonight.

2

For Christ is born of Mary
And, gathered all above,
While mortals sleep,
the angels keep
Their watch of wondering love.
O morning stars, together
Proclaim the holy birth,
And praises sing to God the King
And peace to all the earth.

3

How silently, how silently
The wondrous gift is given!
So God imparts to human hearts
The blessings of his heaven:
No ear may hear his coming,
But in this world of sin
Where meek souls will receive him, still
The dear Christ enters in.

4

O holy Child of Bethlehem,
Descend to us, we pray:
Cast out our sin, and enter in,
Be born in us today!
We hear the Christmas angels
The great glad tidings tell:
O come to us, abide with us,
Our Lord Emmanuel!

PHILLIPS BROOKS (1835–93)